St TERESA.

THE
EXCLAMATIONS
OF THE
SOUL TO GOD;
OR THE
MEDITATIONS
OF
St. Teresa
AFTER COMMUNION.

NEWLY TRANSLATED.

Together with an
INTRODUCTORY DEDICATION
TO A
REVEREND PRIORESS.

BY THE
Rev. John Milner,
Fellow of the Society of Antiquaries.

LONDON;
Printed by J. P. COGHLAN, No. 37. Duke-Street, Grosvenor-Square; and Sold by Messrs. Robinsons, Pater-Noster Row. M,DCC,XC.

TO THE REVEREND MOTHER

MARY AUGUSTINA MORE,

PRIORESS

OF THE

ENGLISH CANONESSES of the ORDER of St. AUGUSTINE at BRUGES.

MADAM,

"*THE Meditations of St. Teresa
"after Communion*" says the pious
and learned Alban Butler, "are full
" of affective sentiments of humi-
" lity, fear, love and other virtues.
" Many sinners, by reading these
" Meditations, have been converted
" to God, and embraced a course

a   " of

"of perfect virtue." *Saints Lives,
vol.* x. *p.* 376. *Nov. Ed.* It was this
testimony of the above mentioned
venerable Author, once the Director
of your pious Community, that first
turned my attention to the present
little treatise. In taking it in hand
I was prepared to meet with those
tender sentiments of devotion, and
those pure maxims of heavenly doctrine, which the Church ascribes to
our Saint in the prayer appointed
for her festival; to my surprize
however, on perusing it, I discovered that pathetic strain of eloquence,
and that quickness and sublimity of
imagination, which are to be found
in few devotional treatises: In short,
I was convinced it deserved to be
generally known, and that it was
not more calculated to gratify the

devotion

devotion of the Pious, than to produce the effect ascribed to it above, by your late respected friend, the conversion of sinners.

Unfortunately however, this work has hitherto, in our tongue, existed only in the cold and obsolete language of Woodhead's literal translation; and owing to some accident, probably to fewer copies of it being taken off, the second Volume of his works of St. Teresa, which contains the present treatise, is extremely scarce. These considerations have induced me to undertake the present work; in which, satisfying myself with preserving the sense of the original, I have taken that liberty with the idiom which seemed necessary to point out the connexion of the Saint's arguments and ideas, and to render the work intelligible and pleasing to an English reader: a mode of translation, which, where controversy is out of the question, appears to me the only one that does justice, at the same time, to the Author and the Reader. With this idea of translating, it will not be expected I should have thought myself under an absolute necessity of working from the original language; it seemed sufficient to ascertain the meaning of the Saint, by versions of approved judgment and fidelity. I therefore consulted and compared together those of the celebrated D'Andilly, the careful F. Cyprian, and our own venerable Woodhead; and finding them almost always agreeing in their sense of the Author, however much they differ in

their

their style of writing, I was persuaded I had every thing that was necessary for my present purpose, and saw the inutility of procuring this translation to be compared with the original Spanish, by persons well skilled in that language, as I had at first designed. The best translation of a devotional treatise in our language (a treatise itself that is not to be equalled in its kind) *The Sufferings of Jesus*, was not made from the original Portuguese, but from the French version of F. Alleaume.

So much for the present translation: As to the reasons which have induced me, Madam, to put it under your patronage, they are such as, I am sensible, I must not mention to you, but, at the same time, they are such as I need not mention

to

to any one elfe, who has the happinefs of being acquainted with you. Thus much however you will allow me to fay, that, in an age which feems to threaten a fecond grand defection from the Church, under the delufive idea of reforming errors and abufes, a work of the old ftamp, like this, calculated to oppofe the prevailing torrent, by oppofing that fpirit of irreligion from which it flows, naturally feeks for protection in a lineal defcendant of that illuftrious Martyr, the Refcuer, in his age, of his country from infamy*, who endeavoured to extinguifh the flames of the firft Reformation with his blood, and whofe Chriftian ufe of the great talents, with which he was entrufted, has proved

* Sir Thomas More.

proved, that men are not always wicked in proportion to the means they have of being so.

There is danger, Madam, to all that is rational and good, from too much speculation and refinement, as well as from stupid ignorance. Hence the Apostle of the Gentiles admonishes us, *not to be more wise than it behoveth to be wise, but to be wise unto sobriety.* Rom. xii. 3. In speaking of the antient Philosophers he had before said, c. i. v. 21, 22. that *they evaporated* * *in their own thoughts . . . . and professing themselves to be wise, they become fools.* The present enlightened age, as it is pleased to term itself, has reasoned, till it has hardly a principle left to reason upon. Politicians have reformed

* Evanuerunt. *Vulg.* εματαιωθησαν. *Gr.*

ed their political conſtitutions, till all the evils of anarchy have poured in upon them. The faſhionable Religioniſts of the day have reformed Chriſtianity, till they have degraded Chriſt himſelf from his throne, and worn down his ſupernatural religion to a ſyſtem that ſtands in need of no Meſſiah at all; and even a great proportion of Catholics themſelves, in the preſent day, are evidently tired of that neceſſary confinement of thought and practice, which is eſſential to their being encloſed in the *one Sheepfold* of the *one Shepherd*, John x. 16. and pant for every kind of Reformation, except that of their morality.

It is now, for the firſt time, the Evangelical Counſels themſelves, not the abuſes of them, are got into

diſrepute

disrepute with an infinite number of Catholics, who have been taught to consider the observers of them as a useless set of beings. We now behold the sacred Cloister invaded, not by the disciples of Calvin or Mahomet, but by the professed children of the Church. We see its peaceful inhabitants stripped of their chartered rights and property, while the privileges of the State are extended to Jews and Idolaters: It is made lawful, in Christian countries, to blaspheme the name of Christ, but not to serve him according to that plan which he himself has pointed out as the most perfect, *Mat.* xix. 21. and to which so many thousands of excellent citizens have sacrificed their fortunes and their lives, under the guarantee of the most solemn public laws.

The present time is also marked by a general combination of Catholics for humbling their Mother Church, in the day of her greateſt diſtreſs, and for ſtripping her of her prerogatives, when ſhe has hardly any other left, than thoſe ſhe has immediately received from the hands of her divine founder. Hence we now behold the common Father of the Faithful conſtantly held up, in writing and converſation, to contempt and hatred, by his own ſpiritual children, and ſometimes even by thoſe, who, like myſelf, have, for years, eaten his material bread; and this on the ſcore of the pretended or exaggerated faults of his predeceſſors, ages before we ourſelves were in being. Hence alſo it is now made a crime of, in the eſtabliſhed Paſtors of the Church, to pronounce when her ſacred rights are invaded; but this queſtion is referred for a ſolution to her profeſſed enemies. In

It is in this age that a general difpofition prevails to remove the land-marks fixed by our fathers, and that we ftudy to unlearn, in polite circles, the awkward leffons we pored over in the ponderous volumes of the Divines and Fathers. The extent of the underftanding is now eftimated by that of the confcience. He who trembles to tamper with the facred conftitution of Religion, muft be contented to pafs for a bigotted narrow-minded man; while the moft fuperficial geniufes will lay claim to fuperior ftrength of underftanding on the mere ftrength of their irreligion. Hence we are told that Afcetical works, of the prefent caft, are no more than the ravings of bigotted Myftics; and hence thofe great and good men, *of whom the world was not worthy*, to whofe zeal and conftancy in fuffering we are indebted

indebted for the sacred deposit of the orthodox faith, instead of Martyrs, as we have hitherto considered them, are now proved to have died Traitors to their country*.

Finally

---

* See *an Answer to the Bishop of Comana's Pastoral Letter*, by a writer who dates from *Moorfields*, and calls himself a *Protesting Catholic*. In this indecent and inflammatory publication, the most bare-faced attempt yet made since the Reformation, to disturb the peace of English Catholics, the writer asserts, that the learned and pious Missioner Mr. Cadwallador, who suffered death at Leominster in 1610 for his Priestly character, but who, like many others of his profession, refused to save his life, by taking the Oath of Allegiance framed by the artful Bancroft and the apostate Perkins, *died a material traitor to his country... and shed his blood for those Papal prejudices we have all disclaimed by the Oath of* 1778. It is plain this very confident writer was ignorant that Mr. Cadwallador, as well as Doctor Bishop

Finally hitherto, we know, the simple and unqualified title of *Catholic* has been

shop of Chalcedon, Dean Colleton, the celebrated Champney, and other sufferers, for refusing the said Oath, actually signed in 1602 a solemn and public Protestation of Allegiance, by which they bound themselves to *support Elizabeth, the reigning Queen, against any foreign Prelate, Prince, or Potentate, in defiance of any Excommunication the Pope might issue against her, or against him, for so doing.* See Dodd, vol ii. p. 292. Miss. Pr. vol. ii. p. 17. On what ground then did these pious and learned men, who, we see, were no slaves to the above mentioned Papal prejudices, principally object to the said Oath? I answer; precisely on that ground on which we object to it at the present day, *viz. the perjury of swearing the erroneous doctrine of the deposing power to be heretical and damnable.* For a proof of the accuracy of this statement, see our late Ven. Challoner's Account Miss. Pr. vol. ii. p. 18. and the remarkable controversy between one of those learned

Priests

been the glory of every member of the Univerfal Church, and has always been brought forward by the Ancient Fathers*, as well as by Modern Controvertifts, as a mark of the Orthodoxy of that Church,

Priefts and Dr. King Bifhop of London, *ibid. p.* 75. and *Dodd, vol.* 2. *p.* 369. It is plain, thofe old-fafhioned Divines did not underftand the morality of fwearing, that to be *herefy in the plain and obvious meaning of the word,* which they underftood to be only *materially* fo. If any difficulty is ftarted concerning the *popular meaning* of the word *Herefy,* let Johnfon be confulted, and the authorities he refers to. It behoves us to take care not to be more afraid of the *infamy* than of the *guilt* of equivocation and deceit!

* St. Pacian fays, "My Name is *Chriftian,*
" my Surname is *Catholic* .... the former title
" is my fignature, the latter the proof of my
" right to that fignature." *Ep.* 1. *ad Symph.*
St. Auguftine alfo fays, *Lib. contra Ep. Manic.*
" The very name of *Catholic...* keeps me in
" the bofom of the Church."

which

which has been able, in all ages, invariably to maintain it simple and unadulterated. But now it seems that many of our Brethren are ashamed of it, or at least unwilling to bear it, unless it is debased and burlesqued, for the crooked purposes of worldly policy, by being united with the distinctive titles of acknowledged Schismatics and Heretics. Till the present day, we have even ridiculed, in our adversaries, the attempt of uniting together the incongruous titles, which we can still hardly pronounce without a smile, of *Protestant Catholics* and *Orthodox Dissenters**.

In short that man must be blind indeed, or deeply infected with the prevailing contagion, who does not
see

---

* The words *Heterodox* and *Dissenter* have actly the same radical meaning.

see that a spirit of irreligion and immorality keeps pace with the present rage for innovation, and that at no period, during near eighteen hundred years the Church has existed, she has worn so melancholy an aspect as at the present moment. But he that has promised to *abide with his Church all days even to the consummation of the world*, Mat. xxviii. 20. has also assured us, that *scandals must necessarily come*; Mat. xviii. 7. as he foretold the encrease so he also foretold the decrease of faith, *Luke* xviii. 8. previous to that great day *when he shall come with his fan in his hand, and shall thoroughly cleanse his floor, gathering the wheat into the barn, but burning the chaff with unquenchable fire*, Mat. iii. 12. then *shall he present* the Church *to himself a glorious Church, not having spot or wrinkle*. Eph. v. 27.

In the description I have just given of the temper of the times, which, I would to God any one could prove to be unfounded or exaggerated in a single particular, there are two charges implied, which I feel myself obliged to meet, in a more direct manner, one that affects the writings, the other the profession of the Saint, whose work I am giving to the Public. I have supposed the following treatise, so far from suiting the taste of many modern Catholics, will be the subject of their ridicule. But in opposition to this, I will venture to assert, that, as far as we can pronounce on the opinion of the Church, where no formal decision has taken place, there are perhaps no writings, that have been more pointedly or more strongly approved of by this unerring Judge, than thofe of St. Terefa. Her fpirit of prayer, and the character of her afcetical works, were not only examined and approved of by the moſt eminent Divines of the age, but alfo by a conſtellation of her holy contemporaries, fuch as St. Francis Borgia, St. Peter of Alcantara, St. John of the Crofs, and St. Lewis Bertrand, who were the beſt, becaufe they were experimental judges of the excellency of her *heavenly doctrine;* for fo it is ſtyled by the Church, as I obferved before, in the prayer inferted in her public liturgy, after a fecond examination of our Saint's fpirit and writings had taken place. It is due to St. Terefa here to mention, that it was not in compliance with her own inclination, but in conformity

conformity with the express orders of her Superiors, she wrote the several edifying treatises she has left behind her. How little there was of art or study in our Saint's writings, and to what degree they were the spontaneous overflowings of her devotion, may be gathered from the extraordinary circumstance related of them, that in the original still extant, there is not a single erasure to be found, and likewise from the following authentic account to be seen in the aforesaid *Saints lives*, vol. x. p. 377. " One night, whilst
" she was writing *these very medita-*
" *tions*, a Nun came into her cell,
" and sat by her a good while in
" great admiration, beholding her,
" as it were, in an enraptured state,
" holding a pen in her hand, but often

" often interrupting her writing,
" laying down her pen, and fetch-
" ing deep fighs: her eyes appeared
" full of fire, and her face fhone
" with a bright light, fo that the
" Nun trembling with awe and re-
" fpect, went out again, without
" being perceived by the Saint."

The defence of the Religious profeffion, now fo much attacked, and every where attacked with impunity, I owe not only to our Saint, who was fo eminent a propagator of it; but alfo to the Lady I am now addreffing, who, like our Saint, has facrificed to it all her worldly profpects, when placed in the dazzling funfhine of youth. But when I profefs myfelf the advocate of this ftate, it is only, where it is embraced upon proper motives, and where the fpirit of it

is

is properly preserved, as envy itself must allow to be the case, with regard, Madam, to your pious Community, and to the edifying inhabitants of our English Convents in general. The only clamor that is, or can be, raised against persons of this description, is, as I have intimated above, that they are of no use to the world. I might here enter into a just and serious enquiry, of what use to the world the generality of those persons are, in whose mouths this objection is more frequently found, and for what beneficial purposes their time from morning till night is professedly spent. But, leaving that enquiry to their own consciences, I answer, if we are Christians, we must be convinced that the salvation of our souls is the

first

first law of nature; now if, amidst the incentives to vice, with which the world abounds, it should appear to certain persons, that a life of retirement and celibacy is necessary, or even useful, for this end, while such persons are obedient to the laws of the Community, and court not its emoluments, why should not they be permitted to do that for virtuous purposes, which others are free to do for purposes of vice?

I am far however from allowing that Religious persons, who possess the true spirit of their calling, are of no advantage to the world. On the contrary, *If we have faith but as a grain of mustard-seed,* Mat. xvii. 19. we must allow, that they are a public benefit and bulwark, were it

only

only on account of the prayers, which they unceasingly pour forth for the temporal and eternal welfare of others. Scripture tells us, that *the constant prayer of the just man availeth much,* Jam. v. 16. and there can be no doubt but, at the great day of retribution, the merit of many a splendid conversion, and of other good works, will be taken from those, who were the immediate instruments in performing them, and given to certain souls, who are now hidden in impenetrable obscurity: there can be no doubt also, but that, it is for the sake of such souls as these, who are held up by worldlings, not only as useless beings, but also *as a parable of reproach, whose life seemeth madness, and their end without honor,* Wisd. v. 3. the judgments of God

are

are suspended over the heads of these very worldlings. Little did the two hundred and seventy five fellow-voyagers of St. Paul suspect, it was for the sake of him, a reputed criminal in chains, that their lives were spared. *Acts* xxvii. Sodom itself would have been saved, had there been but ten just persons in it. *Gen.* xviii. And Christ promised, that those days of desolation he spoke of in St *Mat.* xxiv. 22. should be shortened, on account of the Elect.

Your profession, Madam, is not useless to the Christian world, while you continue to edify it by your example. It is of the utmost consequence to the cause of Christianity, so intimately connected with the temporal welfare of mankind,

that

that Religion should be protected in its genuine perfection, and that it should have certain retreats, where it may exert its full influence, the thorns being, as it were, plucked up that usually prevent its due growth. Now it would be madness to say, that the retirement of the Cloister has not, in all ages, been found more favorable for this purpose than a situation amidst *the cares, and riches, and pleasures of this life.* Luke vi. 14. Corrupted as we are by our mutual intercourse, and by the infatuating customs, language and amusements of the world, there is reason to fear we might think the sublime and self-denying morality of the Gospel to be mere matter of speculation, and Platonic reveries, did not we see it frequently realized by the heroic sacrifices and conduct, chiefly of those who have retired to breathe the pure air of the Cloister, and with *Mary have chosen the better part.*

Finally, Madam, your Religious Houses are not only useful, but, I may say, necessary for the proper education of female youth; at least this is certain with respect to the Catholic female youth of this kingdom. It is true, the latter are, as a celebrated Catholic writer of the present day, expresses it*, *the forlorn hope of the Catholic cause.* In fact the incentives to libertinism and irreligion are, in this day, so numerous and violent with regard to the

* See *the State and Behaviour of the English Catholics, from the Reformation to the Year* 1780. p. 180.

youth of our sex; it would be so unfashionable and un-gentleman-like, as well as so inconvenient, in them, to betray an awe of the truths of faith or the precepts of morality, that it is not extraordinary we should place our chief dependance, for the Religion of the future generation, on the piety and decorum of the youth of your sex. But where are they, with God's assistance, to acquire these invaluable advantages, except where their mothers have acquired them, in the advantages and spirit of a Convent education?

The writer I have just quoted, who perhaps sometimes deals in paradox, in order to exercise the powers of his eloquence in rendering it plausible, and who certainly

possesses

possesses a brilliancy of talents sufficient to enliven the gravest subjects, without those sallies of levity, and sometimes irreligion, with which he disgraces them; this writer, I say, himself of the clerical order, at the same time that he allows the Catholic Ladies, who have been educated in Convents, *to stand unrivalled as Wives, Mothers, Citizens, and Christians**, asserts, *that Nuns are ill adapted to the business of educating them,* and that *no mode of education can be less adapted to improve the mind, and instil such principles as may form it to the business of life, than that which these unrivalled ladies have actually received.* This to me is indeed a paradox, unless we are to under-

---

* See *pages* 180, 181, of the above mentioned un-equal performance.

ſtand literally, what this Gentleman advances concerning *the too great partiality of nature* in having beſtowed more elements upon the Catholic Ladies than fell to their ſhare, and which therefore may be ſuppoſed to have ſupplied for the defects of their education. But, jeſting apart; I would aſk this intelligent Author, whether in the many Convents he is acquainted with, ſome of which are ornamented with his own neareſt relatives, there are not Ladies now under the veil every way equal to thoſe in the world; Ladies, who, with firſt-rate talents, have had every opportunity of improvement and obſervation, which an elevation of birth and ſituation could afford? and whether theſe are not the perſons to whom the de-

partment

partment of education is mostly assigned in our Convents? But the principal question I wish to ask him is, what *those principles* are which he considers as requisite to *form the female mind for the discharge of the important duties of Wife, Mother, Citizen and Christian,* and which a Convent education cannot instil? and whether he wishes to substitute the elegant Boarding Schools of the day, with all their fund of fashionable knowledge, instead of our antiquated Cloisters? As far as I can judge, the above mentioned principles lie within a very narrow compass, and are precisely those which the Convent education is peculiarly calculated to instil; they may be comprized in a word, a sacred attachment to religion and morality,

lity. It is evidently impossible to conceive a Lady, in any of the aforesaid situations, to be deficient in her duty, on whose mind virtue and piety have taken this firm hold. As to that knowledge of the world which is requisite for the due exercise of these qualities; when it becomes necessary, we know it is very soon acquired; and to learn it prematurely, is evidently to risk the attainment of the qualities themselves. The Author seems to allow the necessity of excluding the incentives to vice and folly, and of retiring from *public notice till maturer age has ripened female virtue to secure perfection*, and even ascribes to this, as a cause, that merit, of which it is evidently only a condition. But where is this lesson practised, where

can

can it generally be practised, except within the Convent walls?

The modern improvers of female education shew themselves ignorant of the distinctive characters of the sexes, no wonder the errors of their plan should appear in the unexampled immorality of their fashionable pupils. It is solid virtue, and unaffected piety, not the trivial accomplishments of the age, that are calculated to promote the good of mankind, and to form domestic happiness; these are what all the world seek for in those they are connected with, however destitute of these qualities they are themselves. The greatest accomplishment a truly respectable woman can now have, is to be totally igno-

rant

rant of one half of modern female accomplishments.

Persevere then, Madam, in the plan, which even those who declare themselves its enemies, allow to have been hitherto successful. Continue to imprint deeply in the minds of those, who have the happiness of being educated under your care, the fear of God, and a horror of the reigning vices and temptations of the world! Make them sensible that virtue forms the basis of female merit; and that modesty adds to it its most attractive charm; Finally, that *Piety is useful for all things, having the promise of the life that is now, and of that which is to come.* 1 Tim. iv. 8.

I remain

I remain, with the sincerest respect, and with the greatest confidence in your good prayers,

MADAM,

Your most obedient and faithful Servant in Christ,

JOHN MILNER.

St. Peter's-House, Winchester,
April 15, 1790.

THE EXCLAMATIONS OF THE SOUL TO GOD. &c.

MEDITATION I.

The Complaint of a Soul, by reason of her Distance from God, in this mortal Life.

O How does this life of mine subsist, at a distance from him who is my true life? What am I doing? What am I capable of doing, in this state of separation from my God? Alas! I can do nothing but what is made up of sin and imperfection. What rest can my soul find in the tempestuous sea of this world? I bewail my present misery, but I bewail still more my former condition when I lived exempt from sorrow. O Lord, how sweet are thy ways! yet who can walk in them without fearful anxiety? I dare not live without endeavouring to serve thee, and when I attempt to acquit myself of this duty, overpowered by the immensity of my obligations to thee, I find nothing that is worthy of thy acceptance. I seem desirous of spending myself in thy service; but when I look well to the miserable state I am in, I feel myself incapable of all that is good, unless thou art pleased first to bestow it upon me.

O my gracious and most merciful God, what shall I do to correspond with the great things thou hast wrought in my behalf! All thy
works

works are holy, juſt, infinitely important, and full of heavenly wiſdom, ſince thou who performeſt them, art the Eſſential Wiſdom; nevertheleſs I experience that while my underſtanding employs itſelf in contemplating theſe works, my affections are reſtrained from indulging themſelves in the unconfined manner they deſire in the ſweet exerciſe of loving thee: In this ſtate, the former ſtrives in vain to reach thee in thy inacceſſible grandeur, and the latter to enjoy thee in the ſtreight priſon of this mortal body. Hence every exterior object becomes irkſome and painful to my ſoul, although at a former period, O my God, I am forced to acknowledge, that the conſideration of thy greatneſs, by which ſhe was enabled to eſtimate

her

her own littleness and imperfection, was of signal service to her.

But why do I repeat all this, O my God? Whom am I complaining to, or who else hears me except thou my Father and my Creator? And what need is there of words to thee, who so manifestly residest in the centre of my soul? Such is my weakness. But alas, O my God, how am I assured of this? How do I know that I am not at this moment deprived of thy grace? O this life of mine, which must necessarily continue in uncertainty, concerning a thing of such infinite importance, as the possession of God's favor. What is there desirable in it, since the only advantage it possesses, that of pleasing God in all things, is in itself of so uncertain and precarious a nature?

MEDI-

MEDITATION II.

On the Pain a Soul suffers, that loves God, between her impatience of possessing him, and her Desire of benefiting other Souls.

I Oftentimes think, O my God, that if any thing can render life supportable to my soul in this state of her banishment, it is solitude, because this enables her to repose in thee, who art her only resting place, yet the incapacity she experiences to enjoy thee in that perfect manner she wishes, often turns this pleasure into pain: but O! how delicious is this very pain, when compared with the irksomeness of conversing with creatures? But tell me, my God, how it is, that even this delicious

solitude

solitude wearies a soul that relishes no pleasure but in thee, when she is called upon to serve her fellow-creatures. O omnipotent love of God, how different are thy effects from from those of carnal love! The latter is fearful of any other persons being inflamed with the same passion, least it should lose something it was possessed of, but the love of my God receives new pleasure and a fresh encrease in proportion to the number of companions it meets with in this sweet exercise; and, on the other hand, it is a bitter allay to its felicity, that any should be found who are strangers to this delight.

This, O my supreme Good, is the cause, that even thy sweetest consolations and caresses overwhelm thy servants with grief in the moment of their enjoying them, while they
reflect

reflect on the great number of Chriſtians that ſlight theſe pleaſures at preſent, and ſhall be deprived of them for ever hereafter. Hence thy ſervants earneſtly ſeek to make others partakers of their felicity, and willingly part with the delights they themſelves experience in order to bring others to an acquaintance with them. But would it not be better, O my heavenly Father, on theſe occaſions, to poſtpone this anxious concern for others to a moment of leſs conſolation and delight, and to employ the preſent happy time entirely in the love and enjoyment of thee! O my Jeſus, how great is the love thou beareſt to the children of men, ſince thou art pleaſed, that the moſt acceptable ſervice we can offer thee, ſhould conſiſt in quitting thy company in

order

order to benefit them, and that this should even be the moſt perfect manner of enjoying thee! It is true, the feelings of the ſoul are leſs delicious at theſe times, yet ſhe comforts herſelf in the accompliſhment of thy bleſſed will; and ſhe is moreover convinced, that however exquiſite and divine the conſolations ſhe enjoys in this mortal life may appear, they are all uncertain and ſuſpicious, if they are not accompanied with thy favourite virtue, the love of our neighbour. Whoever loves not his neighbour, loves not thee, O God; and how dear each one of us is to thee, the torrents of blood thou haſt ſhed for him will beſt declare.

MEDITATION III.

Sentiments of a Penitent Soul in the Confideration of her Sins, and of the Mercies of God.

WHEN I reflect, O my God, on the glory thou haft prepared for thofe who perfevere in thy holy fervice, on the labors and pains thy eternal Son has endured to purchafe this glory for us, on our abfolute unworthinefs of it, and on the ingratitude it would imply to neglect correfponding with that love which has exerted itfelf in fo wonderful a manner in our regard, when I confider all this, my foul is overwhelmed with affliction. For how is it poffible, O Lord, that mankind fhould forget all this, as they prove

by

by their readiness to offend thee? How is it possible they should forget themselves and their own interest in the manner they do? But such, O my Redeemer, is the excess of thy bounty, that in the very moment in which we destroy our own souls by aiming a mortal blow at thee, thou art mindful of us, thou overlookest our ingratitude, thou stretchest out thy hand to preserve us, thou awakenest us from our dreadful phrensy, and teachest us to petition thee for the remedy of our evils. O! blessed be this gracious Lord, blessed be his infinite mercy, blessed for all eternity be his tender compassion. O my soul, do thou for ever bless this adorable God. How can any Christians be found to rebel against him! O, how does their ingratitude stand condemned by the excefs of his goodnefs! Do thou, my Saviour, put a final ftop to this ingratitude.

O ye Sons of Men, how long will you continue to be hard of heart? How long will you ftand in oppofition to your meek and loving Saviour? What means this folly? Can you continue to oppofe him to the end? No, this cannot be; for the life of man decays like the flowers of the field, and the Son of the Virgin fhall finally come to pronounce the dreadful fentence of your eternal fate. O my omnipotent God, fince, whether we are willing or not, thou muft be our judge, why do not we confider beforehand, how much it imports us to render thee propitious to us againft that hour of terror? And yet, after all, who would wifh, my God, to

have

have any other judge of his fate than thee? Thrice happy they who, at that dreadful time, shall be enabled to rejoice with thee!

O my Lord and my God, how is it that a Christian, whom thou hast raised from the abyss of sin, who sees the miserable condition to which he had reduced himself for a momentary satisfaction, and who is resolved, by the assistance of thy grace, which is never wanting to those who love thee, and who persevere in petitioning for the gift of an inviolable fidelity to thee, how is it that such a one can by any means support life! How can he avoid dying with grief at the reflection of what he lost in losing his baptismal innocence! The happiest life that such a Christian can lead, is to be continually dying with this reflection.

flection. Yet by what means can a soul, that tenderly loves thee, support itself in this state? Alas, my God, whither are my thoughts straying! Can I then forget that thou camest into the world to redeem sinners? Can I forget, at how dear a price thou hast redeemed them? Yes, my Saviour, thou hast expiated my false pleasures by real pains and bloody stripes? Thou hast cured my interior blindness by the hood-winking of thy sacred eyes, and thou hast atoned for my vain-glorious thoughts, by the sharp and cruel thorns with which thy blessed head was crowned. O my Lord, my dearest Lord, the consideration of all this torments the more a soul that loves thee: the only consolation I find under this reflection is, that thy mercy shall be the more
extolled,

extolled, in proportion as my wickedness shall hereafter be more fully discovered. Yet shall not this torment ever entirely cease, until, with every other misery of this mortal life, it shall be forgotten in the sight and enjoyment of thee.

MEDITATION IV.

A Prayer, that God would enable us to redeem the Time we have spent otherwise than in his love and service.

IT seems, O my God, that my soul enjoys a certain repose in the consideration of the joy it shall experience, if through thy mercy it should come to the possession of thee; but, in the mean time, it is

my

my earnest desire to serve thee, since it was by serving me thou hast acquired that happiness which I hope to enjoy. What shall I now do, O my Lord? What shall I do? for alas, too late do I experience this desire of serving thee, notwithstanding that in the earliest part of my life thou didst seek to gain me, and didst call upon me to give myself entirely to thee. But hast thou ever yet rejected any soul, on account of its misery? Or hast thou turned a deaf ear to any one that called for thy mercy? Have any limits yet been found for the extent of thy goodness and thy power? Now then, O my most merciful God, is the time to display these attributes in regard to this thy supplicating servant, by inspiring me with a contrition for the

loss

loss of so much precious time as I have misspent in my past life, and in enabling me, O my God, to redeem it. It may seem a folly to ask this favor of thee, since every one agrees, that past time cannot be recovered. But blessed be thou, my God and my Saviour, whose power is infinite, and to whom nothing is of course impossible, do thou only will it, my God, do thou only will it, and however imperfect is my faith, I believe it will be done. The more I reflect on the wonders thou hast performed, and the still greater thou art capable of performing, the more is my faith strengthened, and the greater confidence do I entertain of thy granting the request I make at present. But after all what is there extraordinary in any thing that proceeds

from

from an Almighty Power? Thou knoweſt, O my God, that in all my ſpiritual miſery I was never wanting in acknowledging the greatneſs of thy power and mercy. Have regard to the grace thou haſt beſtowed upon me in preſerving me from offending thee at leaſt in this particular. Recover then for me, O God, the time I have loſt, by beſtowing on me a more plentiful effuſion of thy grace, ſo that, late as it is, I may yet provide, againſt thy coming, that nuptial garment which is neceſſary to entitle me to a ſeat at thy heavenly banquet. If thou wilt, O Lord, this ſhall certainly be done.

MEDITATION V.

On Martha's complaint of Mary, Luke, c. x. and how justly a soul that loves God may complain to him of her present miseries.

O My dearest Lord, how can that soul, which has been so ungrateful to thee, and has made so bad a use of past favors, presume to demand fresh favors at thy hands? Can that person be trusted, whose treachery has been so often proved before? But what then shall I do in these extremities, O thou comfort of the afflicted, and refuge of those who put their trust in thee? Had I better conceal my wants, until thou thyself shalt, unsolicited, relieve them? No, most certainly, because thou,

thou, my Lord, and my Delight, knowing how numerous, and how pressing they are, and likewise the consolation it affords me to bewail them in thy presence, hast commanded us, on all such occasions, to offer up our petitions to thee, with a full assurance of thy granting what we ask for.

I sometimes think of the complaint which holy Martha made to thee; for she seems to me, not so much to have blamed her sister, as to have lamented, that thou didst not attend to the pains she took to please thee, and that thou didst not seem desirous of her continuing near thy divine person. She probably thought she was not so much beloved by thee as her sister was, and she certainly must have been much more sensible of this misfortune, than of the pains it coſt her in ſerving thee who wert ſo dear to her. For this her love of thee could not but render ſuch labors delightful to her. This appears farther, from her not addreſſing herſelf to her ſiſter, but only to thee, O Lord; her love emboldening her to aſk of thee, *If thou hadſt no care of her?* Thy anſwer alſo points out the purport of her complaint, in giving her to underſtand, that it is love alone which gives a value to whatever we do, and that the *one thing neceſſary* is to love thee in ſuch manner, as that nothing may ever interrupt the exerciſe of this love.

But how can we obtain a love that ſhall correſpond with what we owe to our beloved? It is impoſſible, O my God, except our love be

united

united with and draw its merit from that infinite love which thou bearest us. Shall I then complain, with this holy woman, that thou doft not sufficiently love and regard me? Alas, my God, I have no cause for so doing; on the contrary, I have ever experienced much stronger and more wonderful proofs of thy love than I have even known how to ask for or desire. If I ought to complain of any thing, it should be that thy mercy has been too great in bearing with my ingratitude. What then can so miserable a wretch as I am ask of thee, unless it be, according to the sentiment of the great St. Augustine, that thou wouldst give me before-hand whatever I am to re-pay to thee; for thus only can I satisfy, for the smallest part of the immense debt I

owe

owe thee. Remember, O my Creator, that I am the workmanship of thy hands, teach me to know thee in order that I may love thee.

MEDITATION VI.

How tedious life is to a soul that ardently desires to be united to her God.

O Thou Lord of all things, my Delight and my God, how long shall I continue languishing to behold thee? What comfort can be afforded that soul which has learned to relish no other but what it finds in thee? O this long life! this tedious life! this dying life, which I lead here upon earth! What a lonesome exile is it, and how destitute of all comfort! How long, O Lord, how long shall it endure! What, O my sovereign

sovereign Good, say, what shall I do whilst it continues? Shall I wish to be delivered from this ardent desire of enjoying thee that torments me? O my Creator and my God, Thou dost give wounds that want no cure, thou dost strike without bruising, thou dost kill, and thereby bestow new life, in fine, thou dost act in all things conformably to the infinitude of thy power, it is thy pleasure, that this contemptible worm of the earth should be the subject of such strange contrarieties! Be it so then, my God, since thou hast so ordained it, for I desire nothing but that thy will may be done in all things. But alas, my Creator, extreme grief makes me speak and complain of that which admits of no remedy, till thou shalt please to provide one. It is true, my soul,

pent

pent up in close bondage, ardently sighs for her deliverance, but even this she only desires in conformity with thy blessed will. Let this pain, O Lord, encrease on earth, by encreasing my love of thee, or else afford me a cure for it in the sight of thee in heaven.

O Death! O Death! where is the Christian that fears thee, since thou alone art the gate of life? But, alas, how can that Christian avoid fearing thee, who has passed the greatest part of his life devoid of the fear and love of his God? And since I am conscious of being in that situation, what is it I pray for in praying for my death? What do I ask for, but perhaps for the punishment I have deserved by my sins? But O thou my only Good, do thou avert this heavy doom from me me, to redeem me from which thou haſt paid ſo dear a price. And do thou, O my ſoul, abandon thyſelf to the holy will of God, ſince this is evidently thy wiſeſt courſe. Serve him during his good pleaſure, and truſt that he will deliver thee from the pains of this exile, when by due penance thou ſhalt have obtained the pardon of thy ſins: do not look for enjoyment till thou haſt merited it by ſuffering: but alas, thou my true Lord and only King, I am utterly incapable even of this, unleſs thou doſt ſtrengthen me for this purpoſe by thy grace: for with thy grace I can do all things.

MEDITATION VII.

On the infinite Goodness of God, who testifies, that his delight is to be with the children of men.

O Thou my true Lord, and only Hope, my Father, my Brother, and my Creator, how does my soul overflow with joy at that comfortable assurance thou haft given us, that thy *delight is to be with the children of men!* Prov. viii. 31. How effectual are these words, O thou sovereign Lord of heaven and earth, to dispel every darksome cloud of despair from the minds of sinners! Is it for the want of an object of thy divine complacency, that thou art delighted with so mean and filthy a worm as I am? No, my God, thou hast pro-

claimed

claimed from heaven, at the baptism of thy Son, that in him *thou art well pleased*, Mat. iii. 17. &c. dost thou then put us upon a footing with him? O incomprehensible mercy! O astonishing favor, so far transcending our deserts! Can we mortals ever forget it? O my God, thou who knowest all things, knowest my misery, and how capable I am of this ingratitude; but do thou mercifully prevent it. And now, my soul, let us think, how great love and complacency the eternal Father conceives in the contemplation of his co-eternal Son, and the Son reciprocally in the contemplation of the Father; think, at the same time, of the inflamed ardor with which the Holy Ghost is united to the Father and the Son, in the contemplation of them; and how these three

three ineffable perfons are infeparably united in this mutual contemplation and love, becaufe they are the fame undivided Deity. Thefe adorable perfons mutually know, mutually love, and mutually delight in each other. What need then have they of my love? Tell me, O my God, why thou doft defire to have it, or what benefit it is of to thee? Bleffed be thou, O my God, bleffed be thou for ever, bleffed be thou by all thy creatures, world without end, becaufe there is neither end nor meafure in thee, or in thy divine perfections. Rejoice, O my foul, that thy God is loved as he deferves to be loved, in as much as his own infinite perfections are the object of his infinite knowledge and complacency. Thank him, that even here on earth he he has been worthily known and loved by his divine Son. Under his protection thou mayeſt approach the divine Majeſty, and preſume to beſeech him that, ſince he deigns to delight in thee, the whole circle of created beings may not have power to prevent thee from delighting in him, and rejoicing in his infinite perfections, and that he is ſo worthy to be loved and praiſed by all his creatures. Beg of him alſo, that he would enable thee to contribute, in ſome degree, to the ſanctification of his holy name, and that thou mayeſt be enabled to repeat, in the ſincerity of thy heart, with the bleſſed Virgin, *My ſoul doth magnify* and praiſe *the Lord.* Luke i. 46.

MEDI-

MEDITATION VIII.

A Prayer for Sinners, who are so insensible of their blindness, that they do not even desire to be enlightened.

O My Lord and my God, how truly *hast thou the words of eternal life,* John vi. 69. wherein we may find whatever we stand in need of, if we will but be at the pains of searching for it. But what wonder is it, if we forget thy sacred words, in that state of folly and spiritual misery into which our sins have cast us? O my God, thou Creator of the Universe, in whose presence all that thou hast yet created is nothing in comparison with what thou art able to create: Thou, omnipotent God, who canst do infinitely

more

more than I am able to underſtand, make me the ſubject of thy infinite power, and grant that thy words may never be effaced from my mind. Thou has ſaid, *Come to me all you that labor and are oppreſſed, and I will refreſh you.* Mat. xi. 28. What can we wiſh for, what can we aſk for more than thou haſt here promiſed us? and why are worldlings loſt but for ſeeking, elſewhere than in thee, for their comfort and repoſe? Alas, my God, how wretched and blind are thoſe who ſeek for repoſe out of thee? Have compaſſion, O Lord, on the creatures thou haſt made: Remember that we are ſtrangers to ourſelves, that we know not what we wiſh for, and that we wander far from the happineſs we are in ſearch of. Give light, O God, to our ſouls. We are in a ſtill more

deplorable

deplorable ſtate of blindneſs than the man born blind was, whom we read of in the Goſpel: for he earneſtly wiſhed and prayed for his ſight, but we are in total darkneſs, and are contented to remain ſo. How deſperate, alas, is our condition! Here, O my God, is need, at the ſame time, of thy omnipotent power, and of thy inexhauſtible mercy. Thou Lord of my heart, and only true God, how great a favor do I now preſume to aſk thee! It is no other than that thou wouldſt deign to love thoſe who do not love thee, that thou wouldſt open to thoſe who do not ſo much as knock, and that thou wouldſt afford a cure to thoſe who are delighted with their malady, and who ſtudiouſly endeavour to encreaſe it. Thou haſt ſaid, my God, that thou didſt come on earth,

to

to call sinners, Mat. ix. 16. These, O Lord, are in the strict sense sinners. Do not have regard to our blindness, but cast thine eyes on the streams of blood thy Son has poured forth for our salvation. Make the light of thy mercy shine forth through the thick cloud of our sinful passions. Consider us, O God, as the work of thy hands, and save us for thy mercy's and bounty's sake.

MEDITATION IX.

Another Prayer to God for those infatuated souls, who are not desirous of being delivered from their spitual maladies.

O God, whose compassion and love for my soul is so great, thou hast also said, *If any one thirst, let him come to me and drink,* John vii. 37. Alas, how can those avoid being thirsty who are burning with the flames of worldly passions? and what copious draughts do they require to prevent their being totally consumed? I know thy bounty is such, that thou wilt not refuse, even to these, thy heavenly water; thou hast promised it, and thy words can never fail. But if, alas, from long

habit

habit, they do not perceive the heat of these flames, but rather cherish themselves with it; if they have so far lost their reason, as to be insensible of their miserable condition, what remedy, O my God, is left for them? Nevertheless thou art come into the world to remedy even such desperate maladies as these are. Enter then, O Lord, upon this work at present. It is in such deplorable cases of misery that the greatness of thy mercy will appear. Consider that these thy enemies are making daily advances in their sinful career. Have pity on those who have no pity on themselves, and since they are so desperately miserable as not to desire to come to thee, do thou, O Lord, condescend to go in search of them. Behold I beg this, in their name,

name, in the full confidence of their rising from the state of death in which they lie at present, as soon as they shall enter into themselves, to know their own misery, and to taste thy sweetness.

O Life, that givest life to all, give me also of this water, which thou hast promised to those who ask for it. Behold I ask for it, my God, and most ardently desire to have it, and I here present myself before thee in order to receive it of thee. Do not withdraw thyself from me, since thou knowest how necessary the solace of thy presence is to a soul that languishes with the love of thee. What a subject of surprize and fear is it, O my God, to consider the different kinds of fire that inflame the breasts of men in this mortal life. The
one

one kind of fire deſtroys the ſoul, and reduces it, as it were, to aſhes; the other purifies, and renders it capable of an immortal life, and of the enjoyment of thee. O wounds of my Saviour, living ſources of grace, how abundantly do you overflow for our refreſhment and preſervation! How ſecurely do they walk amidſt the dangerous fires of this world, who are ever careful to refreſh their ſouls with the ſacred ſtreams flowing from them!

MEDITATION X.

On the small number of the true servants of God. Another Prayer for hardened souls, who refuse to come forth from the sepulchre of their sins.

O GOD of my soul, how forward are we ever to offend thee, and how still more ready art thou to forgive us! Whence, O God, can this daring boldness of ours proceed? If it is from the knowledge we have of the greatness of thy mercy, can we be ignorant, that the extent of thy justice is proportioned to it? Thou hast said, my God, by the mouth of thy Prophet, *The pains of death have encompassed me.* Pf. cxiv. 3. Alas! Alas! how dreadful a thing must sin then be, which
was

was capable of causing torments and death to a God! and does not this cruel persecution, O my God, still pursue thee? Where canst thou go but the sins of men still attack thee, and renew thy wounds with mortal violence?

O Christians, it is at length time for you to take part with him who is your King, and to attend upon him in the general dereliction he experiences: for how small is the number of those that remain faithful to him! while the multitude, that follows the standard of Satan, is great beyond conception. But the worst circumstance of all is, that those, who pretend in public to take part with Jesus, betray him in private, so that he can scarcely find any in whom he can confide. O thou, our only true Friend, how ill do

such

such traitors requite thy friendship and bounty! O ye true Christians, whoever you are, join your tears with those of your Saviour, since he did not shed tears alone for Lazarus, when he wept over his tomb, but likewise for all those, who, though called like him, with a loud voice, yet, unlike him, refuse to quit the grave of their sinful habits. O thou my sovereign Good, how intimately present were my sins at that moment to thy mind! but now at least, O my God, I beseech thee, put a final stop to their course, and not to the course of my sins only, but to the sins of all mankind. Give life to all souls that are dead in sin, and let thy cry, O my Saviour, be so strong, and so efficacious, that it may give life to them, though they do not desire this favor, and may

make

make them finally quit the tomb of their sinful habits. Lazarus himself did not pray to be restored to life, but thou didst work this miracle, at the entreaty of a woman that had been a sinner: behold here, O Lord, is a sinful woman at thy feet, but much more loaded with sins than Magdalen was. Make the greatness of thy mercy, O my God, appear. I ask this mercy, miserable as I am, for those who will not ask it for themselves. Thou knowest, O my sovereign Lord, how much it afflicts me, to reflect on the dreadful torments they must for ever endure, if they are not converted to thee.

O you, who are habituated to the indulgence of ease, comfort, and delight, and who know not what it is to suffer the contradiction of your will

will in any thing, have pity on yourselves. Remember that the day is coming, which shall subject you to the tyranny of the infernal spirits. Consider well, that the Judge, who will then condemn your obstinacy, now entreats you to be converted. Reflect, that you are not sure of a moment of your present life: why then are you such enemies to yourselves, as to refuse eternal life hereafter. O the hardness of the hearts of men! do thou, my God, soften them, by an effort of that mercy which knows no bounds.

MEDITATION XI.

On the dreadful condition of a soul that, at the moment of death, finds herself condemned to eternal torments.

O My good, my gracious God, how is my soul overwhelmed with anguish, when I represent to myself, the condition of one, who, here on earth, has always been respected, beloved, and honored, when at the instant of his passage to the other world, he sees himself utterly lost, and clearly understands, that the torments to which he is doomed shall never have an end! He cannot now shut his eyes to the truths of religion, as he has heretofore done. It appears to him, that he was snatched

snatched from his worldly enjoyments, the very inſtant after he had attained them; ſince whatever paſſes with time will then appear to him momentary. He ſees himſelf ſurrounded with the hideous and pitileſs companions of his endleſs miſery. He feels himſelf plunged into that ſtinking lake, where the infernal dragons ſhall ſtrive which can moſt torment him. In fine, he finds himſelf buried in this darkſome abyſs, which affords nothing but a ſmoaky flame, ſufficient to make him ſee the objects of terror with which he is ſurrounded.

Alas, how infinitely ſhort does the horror of this deſcription fall of the reality! and who, O Lord, has ſo blindfolded this unhappy ſoul, that ſhe does not ſo much as perceive this infernal abyſs, till ſhe
finds

finds herself plunged into it for ever? Who, O Lord, has so shut her ears, that she has never heard what has been a thousand and a thousand times repeated to her, concerning the greatness and the duration of these torments? O never-ending life of woe! O torment without end! O torment without end! how comes it that those who are so sensible of pain, as not to be able to sleep on a bed that is harder than they are accustomed to, should not be afraid of this extremity of sufferings?

O Lord, how do I bewail that unhappy time, when these truths were hidden from my eyes, as they are now from the eyes of so many others! but since thou knowest my extreme affliction at beholding this
unhappy

unhappy multitude, what I entreat of thee is, that thou wouldſt at leaſt open the eyes of ſome one amongſt them, who, by thy grace, may be enabled to give light to the reſt. I do not aſk this favor of thee, for my own ſake, for I am utterly unworthy of every favor at thy hands; but I aſk it through the infinite merits of thy beloved Son. Caſt thine eyes, O God, on his wounds, and ſince he forgave thoſe who inflicted theſe wounds upon him, do thou alſo, O Lord, forgive the ſins we have committed againſt thee.

MEDITATION XII.

How timid we are in serving God, and how bold we are in offending him. A warm exhortation to sinners to enter into themselves.

O My God, and my only Support, how comes it that, being so fearful of consequences in other undertakings, we are only bold and fearless in opposing thee? It seems as if all the children of Adam were confederated in this unnatural warfare. But were not their reason darkened by sin, they would see the folly of attacking him who made them, and of constantly daring him to combat, who in a moment could plunge them into the bottomless abyss. But being blind as they are, they act like

madmen

madmen purſuing their deſtruction, while they think they are contributing to their welfare, and in ſhort oppoſing every maxim of common ſenſe. What remedy is there, O my God, for thoſe who labour under this dreadful infatuation. It is ſaid, that frenzy gives ſtrength to the weakeſt perſons: ſuch at leaſt is the caſe with theſe, O my God, they are weak in every other attempt, and only ſtrong in attacking thee their beſt friend and benefactor.

O incomprehenſible Wiſdom, thou haſt need of all that infinite love thou beareſt us to ſupport ſuch extravagant folly on our part, and patiently to wait till we return to our ſenſes, whilſt, in the mean time, thou provideſt a thouſand remedies to effect our cure.

It

It fills me with aſtoniſhment, O my God, that mankind ſhould be found ſo deſtitute of reſolution, when it is neceſſary to break through the ſlighteſt occaſion of ſin, or to diſengage themſelves from a danger which expoſes them to everlaſting perdition; for, on theſe occaſions, they think it impoſſible to do what is required of them, even though they were ever ſo much deſirous of it, and yet at the ſame time that theſe men ſhould be found ſo ſtrong and reſolute in attacking thy tremendous Majeſty by ſin. Whence is it, O my only Good, that they derive this courage? It cannot be from the captain they follow in this warfare; for he is thy ſlave, and chained down by thee in unquenchable flames. How can he, that is himſelf ſubdued, inſpire others with confidence

confidence to wage war againſt thee? How, on the other hand, can mortals enliſt themſelves in the ſervice of ſuch a maſter, who being driven from his celeſtial inheritance ſuffers the moſt abject ſtate of want? What can he give his followers, who has no other poſſeſſion but endleſs torments? How comes it, O my Creator, how comes it that we are ſo forward to oppoſe thee, and ſo backward in reſiſting Satan? for though we were under no obliga- to thee, our ſovereign Benefactor, and, on the other hand, were indebted for ſomething to the Prince of Darkneſs, yet how could we bring ourſelves to forfeit the true and never-failing rewards thou haſt promiſed us, for the falſe and deluſive joys that he holds out to us? and what dependance can we place

upon

upon his promises to us, who has proved himself a traitor to thee?

O my Lord, how strange is our blindness! O my King, how dreadful is our madness! O my God, how intolerable is our ingratitude! to pay homage to the Devil with the very gifts of thy bounty! to requite thy tender love with bestowing our affections on him who hates thee, and shall hate thee for all eternity! and, after all the blood thou hast shed, the stripes thou hast born, and the other bitter torments thou hast endured for the love of us, instead of avenging the cause of thy heavenly Father (for as to thyself, O my Jesus, thou disclaimest all vengeance, and prayest for thy tormentors) that after all this, I say, we should associate ourselves, and join with those who have thus barbarously

rously treated thee! But since we, at present, follow the same infernal chieftain that they do, who can doubt of our being classed with them hereafter, and of our being the companions of their everlasting torments? This must be the case, unless thy mercy, O Lord, intervenes, by restoring us to our senses, and curing us of our folly.

Return then, O ye children of men, return to yourselves. Cast your eyes on this your King, while yet he is meek, and is disposed to treat you with mercy. Cease to sin, and, on the contrary, turn all the forces of your soul against that infernal foe who is carrying on a fatal war against you, and who is endeavouring to rob you of your heavenly inheritance. Again I say to you, return to yourselves. Open your

your eyes, and, with loud cries and tears, beg light of him who comes to give it to all the world. In the name of God reflect, that by your sins, you aim at his life, who has suffered death to afford life to you, and who alone defends you from all your enemies. But if all this is not sufficient to make you desist from sinning, know that it is in vain you raise yourselves up against his infinite power; and that sooner or later you must atone for this contempt and boldness in unextinguishable flames. Is it because you see, as it were, the hands of this omnipotent Lord tied fast by the love he bears you that you thus insult him? What other than this was the conduct of his executioners, who first bound him with cords, and then proceeded

ceeded to inflict stripes and wounds without number upon him?

O my God, is it possible thou shouldst endure so much for those who are so little sensible of thy sufferings! but the day shall come, O Lord, when thy justice shall in its turn be displayed, and when men shall see if it is not equal to thy mercy. Think of this, Christians, O think of it seriously. It is certain, that we can never comprehend the extent of our obligations to the Almighty, nor the infinitude of his mercy. If then it be true, that his justice is every way equal to his mercy, alas, my God, alas, what shall become of those who have deserved to experience it in all its extent, and who shall be the eternal victims of its severity!

MEDITATION XIII.

On the happiness of the Saints in heaven, and on the folly of mortals in preferring false pleasures at present to this real felicity hereafter.

O Ye holy souls, who now enjoy compleat felicity in heaven without the danger of ever losing it, and who are for ever absorpt in the praises of my God, how happy is your lot! how just is it that you should incessantly pour yourselves forth in this sweet exercise! how does my soul envy your happy condition, freed as you are from the pain of beholding, on one hand, the offences that in this wicked world are each moment committed against my God, and the ingratitude of men towards him, and on the other, their ſtupid inattention to the multitude of ſouls which Satan each day precipitates into hell.

O happy ſpirits, that now enjoy the bliſs of paradiſe, have compaſſion on our miſery, and intercede for us to the Almighty, that he would beſtow upon us ſome ſmall ſhare of your felicity, and that he would dart upon our ſouls one ray of that divine knowledge with which you are wholly enlightened. O my God, make us ſenſible how great the recompence is which thou haſt prepared for thoſe who courageouſly fight thy battles during the dream of this mortal life. O ye ſpirits, all inflamed with love, obtain that we may underſtand, how delightful an employment it is to you, to look forward to that eternity of your
enjoyment

enjoyment of God, and to be convinced, that this your happiness shall never have an end. How wretched are we, O my Saviour, who though we believe these truths, yet for want of reflecting upon them, are so habituated to our blindness, that we neither see them, nor even wish to see them!

Deluded mortals! you who so eagerly pursue your present interest and pleasure, see what you lose by your impatience: perhaps, for want of waiting a single year, a single day, a single hour, or even a single minute, you sacrifice infinite and eternal joys to a wretched momentary gratification. Alas, my God, how little confidence do we repose in thee, since we refuse to wait so short a time for the accomplishment of thy promises! and yet, how much confidence haſt thou placed in us, in intruſting us with the rich treaſure of thy divine Son, during the three and thirty years of his mortal life; as likewiſe with the merits of his bitter death on the croſs! and theſe benefits, O my God, thou didſt provide for us before our birth, and notwithſtanding the foreſight thou hadſt of the ill return we ſhould make thee for them, to the end that nothing might be wanting to us on thy part, towards making us compleatly rich in heavenly treaſures.

O ye happy ſouls, who have made ſo wiſe a uſe of theſe ineſtimable treaſures as to purchaſe with them an inheritance of everlaſting joys, inſtruct us, by your example, to employ them for the ſame bleſſed purpoſe. Obtain for us theſe treaſures, you

you who are so near to their fountain head: draw for us of this heavenly water, O draw, for us, who are here perishing with thirst.

MEDITATION XIV.

On the Countenance of Jesus Christ at the last Judgment, how full of comfort it shall be to the just, and of terror to the wicked.

O My true Lord and my God, he who knows thee not loves thee not; how serious a truth is this! and wo to them who do not take pains to know thee! The hour of death is indeed an hour of terror, but how far more terrible will that last day be, when thy justice shall be executed in its full extent! O my sweet Saviour, I often think what comfort and delight thy eyes will dispense to those who love thee; and on whom thou art pleased to cast a favorable look. Methinks one of these gracious looks, on those thou art pleased to consider as thy own, would be a sufficient recompense for all the years they may have spent in thy service. How hard, my God, is it to make those comprehend this, who have never *tasted how sweet the Lord is!* Think, O Christians, think that you have been raised to the dignity of Brethren of Jesus Christ. Consider him well, and do not despise him, for in proportion to the sweetness of his aspect at that great day, in regard to those who love him, such shall be the terror of his countenance to those who have

opposed

opposed and persecuted him, their Sovereign and their Creator, with all the senses of the body and all the faculties of the soul.

Thou knowest, O my Lord, that I have often been much more terrified at the apprehension of beholding thy countenance incensed against me at the last terrible day, than at the idea of all the torments and furies of hell represented to my mind; and thou knowest how often I have besought thee, as behold, prostrate before thee, I beseech thee now at present, that, of thy infinite mercy, thou wouldst spare me this greatest and most deplorable misery: for what misfortune can befal me equal to this? May every other calamity thou art pleased to appoint overwhelm me, only spare me this, and grant that I may not be be excluded for ever from the sight of thy gracious countenance. Behold thy heavenly Father has bestowed thee as a present upon us, grant that I may not for ever lose thee, my most invaluable treasure. O eternal Father, I confess that I have hitherto been negligent, and faithless in preserving it, but my evil is not without remedy, as long as the period of my trial is not concluded.

O ye, my brethren, my brethren, children of the same common Father with myself, let us exert ourselves to obtain his favor, since he has assured us, that in whatever day we are truly contrite for our offences, he will remember them no more. O boundless mercy of my God, what can we desire more than this? might not we even blush,

without

without such an assurance, to ask for the pardon of our sins upon such terms as these? Let us at least accept of the proffered mercy of our compassionating God, and since he is graciously pleased to court our friendship, let us not refuse it on our part, seeing that he has shed the last drop of his precious blood, and given his life a sacrifice to prove the sincerity of his friendship in our regard. Think also, that he asks nothing at our hands, but what it is infinitely for our advantage to give him. O my God, I am confounded when I consider the insensibility, the blindness, and the stupidity of mankind in this particular: the loss of the most trifling thing, that makes either for our profit or our pleasure, affects us with grief, and yet we can

lose

lose thee, the Majesty of heaven, and together with thee our title to the bright kingdom above, the kingdom of immortal joys, without sorrow or concern! Who can account for this, my God? who can account for it? It is far beyond my comprehension, but do thou, O Lord, I beseech thee, do thou put an end to this extravagant madness.

MEDITATION XV.

On the only confolation of the foul, during its banifhment here on earth.

ALAS, O my God, alas, how long and tirefome is this time of my banifhment, and how much do I fuffer through my impatience to behold thee! O what comfort can the poor foul find, while pent up in the narrow prifon of this mortal body! Men fay that life is fhort, but O how long do I find it. It is fhort indeed, compared with the eternity of blifs which we may fecure by employing it aright; but O, how long does it appear to the foul that impatiently defires to behold

hold her God! What remedy, my God, canst thou apply to this my affliction? there is no other than what arises from the consciousness of my suffering in compliance with thy holy will. O happy affliction, which art the only consolation of a soul that loves her God, do not spare me, since at the same time thou encreasest, thou assuagest the pain which I feel from the absence of my beloved. Lord, all my desire is to please thee, and I am fully convinced that I shall never find content in any thing out of thee; No wonder then I should thus impatiently long for thy presence. Nevertheless if, by my continuance in this life, I can in any degree promote thy divine service, behold me here ready to accept, in imitation

of

of thy holy fervant St. Martin, of whatever labors or fufferings thou fhalt pleafe to ordain for me. But alas, my Saviour, how great is the difference between him and me! He had works to fhew, but I have nothing but words; for indeed I am fit to produce nothing elfe; but do thou, O Lord, have regard to my defires, and not to my merits. Grant, that we may all attain to the love of thee, and fince we muft live our deftined time, let us live for thee alone. May all other defires and all other interefts now ceafe: for what greater gain or what greater pleafure can there be than to pleafe thee!

O thou my God, and my only delight, what can I do to pleafe thee? all the fervice I can render thee is imperfect

imperfect and nothing worth. To what end then do I remain in this miserable life? for no other, my God, except that thy holy will may be accomplished in me. And what can be more for my advantage than this? Wait then, my soul, wait with patience, since thou knowest neither the day nor the hour of thy deliverance. Watch carefully, since every thing here on earth is passing quickly away. It is only thy impatience, that makes what is certain appear doubtful, and what is short appear long. Consider that the longer thou fightest the battles of the Lord, the more thou shewest thy love to him, and the more compleatly thou shalt enjoy his perfections in bliss that shall never end.

MEDITATION XVI.

That God alone is capable of solacing those souls, which he has wounded with the dart of his heavenly love.

O My Lord and my God, it is a great consolation to a soul that suffers, in her absence from thee, to know that thou art present every where. But of what service is this truth to her, when the ardor of her love to thee, O my God, encreases, and the violence of her pain redoubles! for then her understanding grows obscure, and her reason confused, so that she becomes quite insensible of this important maxim;
the

the only thoughts that then poffefs her, are, that fhe is unfortunately feparated from thee, and that fhe can no where difcover a remedy for her calamity. For the heart, that is deeply wounded with divine love, feeks for no counfel or comfort but from him that has inflamed it, knowing that it is from him alone it can receive the affuagement of its pain. When thou pleafeft, O my Saviour, thou doft prefently heal the wound thou haft made, but till then it in vain to look for any remedy or comfort, but in the knowledge of our fufferings anfwering fo good an end.

O Thou, true lover of our fouls, with what goodnefs, with what fweetnefs, with what delight, with what heavenly careffes, with what
demonftrations

demonstrations of an infinite love dost thou cure our wounds, by means of the same love that has caused them! O my God, thou only Comforter of my pains, how foolish is it in me to imagine, that human remedies can sooth a breast that is on fire with the love of thee! Who can penetrate to the depth of this wound of love? who can tell from whence it comes, or how at once a pain so severe and yet so delicious, can be removed? how can it be expected that a wound, inflicted by the Almighty, should be closed by the contemptible efforts of human art?

It is with reason the Spouse, in the Canticles, says, *My Beloved to me, and I to my Beloved,* Cant. ii. 16. She says first, *My Beloved to me,* be-

cause

cause it is not possible, that so divine a thing, as this happy union is, should take its beginning from so base an origin as my affections are. But why, O thou spouse of my soul, if my affections be so base, why do they not rest in creatures? why do they constantly mount up to the Creator? how comes it also to be said, *I to my beloved,* no less than *My beloved to me?* It is thou indeed, my true lover, that dost begin this sweet contest of love, which is first carried on by a total absence of all the powers of my soul, whilst they impatient seek after thee: thus resembling the spouse in the Canticles, by running, as it were, through the streets and public places, and conjuring the daughters of Jerusalem to indicate to them where they can

can find their God. But this contest of love being once begun, against whom do these powers of my soul strive, but against him who has taken possession of that fortress of the soul which they before held, and, who in subduing them, has only in view, that they should be forced to acknowledge their own misery and insufficiency when deprived of him; and thus, by taking from him the graces they stand in need of, they should, in some sort, subdue again their Conqueror? for, by thus renouncing all confidence in their own strength, they derive an effectual strength from him, and in confessing themselves conquered they become truly conquerors. O my soul, what an admirable conflict of this nature hast thou sustained!

and how strictly has the saying of the spouse in the Canticles, *My beloved to me, and I to my beloved,* been verified in thy regard! Who will now attempt to extinguish these united flames, which in fact are no longer two fires but one.

MEDI-

MEDITATION XVII.

That we are ignorant of what we ought to beg of God as conducive to our happiness. The ardent desire of the soul to enjoy the liberty of the children of God, which consists in an exemption from the possibility of offending him.

O My God, Thou infinite and unbounded Wisdom, beyond whatever the understanding of men or angels can possibly conceive! O Love, that dost love me beyond whatever affection I am capable of bearing to myself or even of comprehending! Why should I wish for any thing except what thou art pleased to appoint? Why should I weary myself with begging for the accomplishment of my desires, since thou alone knowest whither these ideas and wishes of mine, would conduct me; whereas I, being ignorant of this, might perhaps find my ruin where I expected to meet with a blessing. If, for example, I ask thee to deliver me from any affliction, thou hast sent me for the purpose of teaching me self-denial, how fatal, evidently, is the nature of such a request? if, on the other hand, I petition for the continuance of such affliction, perhaps I ask for more than my stock of patience, which thou knowest how slender it is, is able to support; and should I actually support it, possibly I might

begin

begin to think that I had done great matters, whereas, in that case, it would be thou that didst perform the whole. If I ask to suffer something for thy sake, perhaps I beg it may not be in such cases; where I am exposed to lose that reputation which I vainly imagine to be necessary for enabling me to promote thy service, flattering myself at the same time, that it is thy honor, and not my own, I am seeking, whereas, after all, perhaps the very means, which I fear might deprive me of the confidence of my fellow creatures, may secure it to me, and enable me to serve thee in a more effectual manner than before, which is the only end I wish to have in view in all things.

I might

I might say much more to the same effect; but thou, O Lord, knowest what I mean better than I do myself. Why then, O Lord, do I employ words at all on this occasion? The reason is, that when the affliction of spirit shall return upon me, and when darkness shall again overspread my soul, I may find myself, as it were, again in this my hand-writing. For oftentimes, O my God, I feel myself so miserable, so weak, and so cowardly, that I seem to look for myself in vain, whom but a little before I seemed to feel endowed with strength and grace enough to encounter all the violence and tempests of the world. Grant, O my God, that I may no more trust in my own imagination, but may thy divine providence dispose of me as it pleases; this I beg, since all my happiness consists in the accomplishment of thy blessed will; whereas if thou wert to grant me all that I myself may wish for, I clearly see that I should bring about my own ruin.

O how short-sighted is the wisdom, and how uncertain the prudence of mankind! do thou, O my God, by thy heavenly wisdom, provide me with the necessary means for serving thee according to thy own will, and not according to mine: Do not inflict the severe punishment upon me, of granting me my requests, when they are not conformable to the designs of thy love, which I wish ever to be the very principle of my life. Let me die to myself, and let one who is great-

er

er than I; who loves me better than I love myself, for ever live in me, that I may learn how to serve him. Let him live in me, and thus give me life; let him reign in me, that thus I may become his servant; for this is the only liberty I crave. Alas, how can that soul be truly free that is not in subjection to the Most High! and what more wretched slavery can she be reduced to, than to lose the protection of her Creator! Happy those who find themselves so strongly bound to thee by the ties of thy love, that it is not in their power to disengage themselves from thee. *Love is strong as death and hard as hell.* Cant. viii. 6. O that we were reduced by it to a state of death, and plunged into this furnace of love without any

hopes

hopes of escaping from it, or rather without any fears of being banished from it! But, alas, O my God, as long as this mortal life endures, we are still in danger for our eternal lot.

O Life, thou enemy of my happiness, why is it not lawful to put an end to thee! I endure thee, because God is pleased to prolong thee, I cherish thee, because thou belongest to him. But do not betray me, nor be ungrateful for the care I take of thee. Yet notwithstanding this, O my God, how am I forced to cry out with the Prophet, *Wo is me, that my banishment is prolonged!* Pf. cxix. 5. It is true, all time is short when considered as the price of eternity, nevertheless one single day, one single hour appears long to the soul that lives in a dreadful uncertainty least she should offend thee.

O thou

O thou free will, how art thou the flave of thyfelf, unlefs thou art ftrongly fixed to thy Creator by the motives of fear and love! O when, fhall that happy day come, when fwallowed up in the abyfs of the Supreme Truth, thou fhalt find thyfelf no longer to poffefs the power of finning, nor wifh to poffefs it, fince then thou fhall feel thyfelf free from all mifery, and happily united with and abforpt in thy God! God is infinitely happy, becaufe he knows himfelf, loves himfelf, and enjoys himfelf without the poffibility of doing otherwife; for could he forget his own attributes, or ceafe to love them, this would not be a perfection but a defect in him: and thou, O my foul, fhalt then enjoy true repofe and happinefs, when thou fhalt be perfectly united with this fovereign Good, and fhalt know

what

what he knows, love what he loves, and enjoy what he enjoys. Then shalt thou no more be subject to change, but thy will shall be immoveably fixed in good, because the grace of God shall act so powerfully in thee, and render thee so perfectly *a partaker of his divine nature*, 2 Pet. i. 4. that thou shalt no longer have it in thy power, or wish to have it in thy power, to forget this Supreme Good, or to cease to enjoy him in transports of love.

Blessed are they whose names are written in the book of immortal life But if thou, my soul, art of that happy number, *why art thou sad, and why dost thou trouble me?* Pf. xli. 6. *Hope in the Lord, because I will yet confess to him,* my sins, and his infinite mercies, and of both together I will make a song of praise mingled with incessant sighs after thee,

thee, *my Saviour and my God. ibid.* It may be a day will come, when, in the regions above, *my glory shall sing to him,* and my conscience be no more *troubled;* Pf. xxix. 13. It is then that sighs and tears shall be no more. In the mean time, *in hope and silence shall my strength be;* If. xxx. 15. I choose rather to live and die in the hope of this happy eternity, than to possess all created beings, and all worldly advantages, which must so soon have an end. Forsake me not, O God, for my trust is in thee: O let me not be confounded for ever. O grant that I may always faithfully serve thee, and in every thing else do with me what thou wilt.

CONTENTS.

www.ingramcontent.com/pod-product-compliance
Ingram Content Group UK Ltd.
Pitfield, Milton Keynes, MK11 3LW, UK
UKHW020654300625
6642UKWH00047B/1263